Dora Incites the Sea-Scribbler to Lament

Geraldine Clarkson

smith|doorstop

Published 2016 by
smith|doorstop Books
The Poetry Business
Bank Street Arts
32-40 Bank Street
Sheffield S1 2DS

Copyright © Geraldine Clarkson 2016
All Rights Reserved

ISBN 978-1-910367-69-8

Designed and Typeset by Utter
Cover photograph: Stephen Clarkson
Printed by Biddles Books

smith|doorstop Books are a member of Inpress:
www.inpressbooks.co.uk. Distributed by Central Books Ltd.,
99 Wallis Road, London E9 5LN

The Poetry Business gratefully acknowledges the support
of Arts Council England.

Contents

5	Biography
6	When they say Connemara,
8	Nuala, Nuala, Nightwatchman's Daughter
9	Write Yourself in Winter
10	A-Man-at- a-Bus-Stop sees a Perfect 'O'
11	Days Round like the Moon
12	'William lets me wear her ring –'
13	The Dazzle and Flash of New Sheets
14	snow rules
16	Queen Conch Ode
17	Hasfallen
18	Goodbye Henna Goodbye
19	Triptych
21	Homily of Francis
22	The thing about Grace and Laura
23	A Less than Sainted Summer
24	Edwardiana
25	Miss Marple loosens her bra,
26	Mise en Gâteau
27	The dancers on graves
28	Bridal
29	caress
30	a young woman undressed me and
31	The Very Skin that Hurts
32	Dora Incites the Sea-Scribbler to Lament
33	the last thing

For my parents, Frances and Frank Clarkson

Biography

I had a red silk cloth for a mother
three gold coins for a father
brothers and sisters were peas
in a pod. We lived at the end of a
stick. Dick was the name of the boy
who led us to fortune.

When they say Connemara,

I hear harebells, wind-flattened,
crouching close to the common.
I hear the gorse-clung mountain
and moorland, bruised
with bottomless ink-lakes
A sequinned Atlantic, waving
to lost relatives in America.

When they mention Murvey
or Ballyconneely – or Calla –
toothless Mary Keeley
blinks at her black doorway,
holding out two tin cans
of buttermilk. I catch the whine
of P.J.'s piano accordion

at dawn, my dead aunts calling
for *Maggie in the Wood* and
Shoe the Donkey and two
fine men to dance a half-set.
Mary Davis stoking up 40 verses
of *The Cleggan Disaster*. My father
unhinging the kitchen door, for leg-room.

When they speak of Ballyruby –
where the monks were –
or slip into the chat news of Erlough
or Dolan, or Horne, my eyes itch
with peat smoke, heather scratches my shins
and I'm barefoot in silt with marsh irises,
hen's crubes and ragged robin.
I'm climbing again the tilted cemetery
at the sea's edge, reclaimed by Dutch clover
and the persistence of rabbits.

When word comes from Gortín or Mannin
(and I'd thought they were all dead there),
or from Seal's Rock – setting the curlews
looping and scraping the sky –
I hear the empty rule of wind
on that thin mile
of white sand, the collapsing
surf, the whistle of silence.

Nuala, Nuala, Nightwatchman's Daughter

Nuanced at first, Nuala brutalised herself after seasons
in the cloister. The finer things belonged on the outside. Nothing
was as it seemed. Where she had envisaged a crucible of white-hot
smoking charity, was cold marble, clipped vowels, and salad bowls.

There was, however, work to be done. Scales of all kinds
to be dealt with – of fish, a glut every day in the kitchen; of tonic sol-fa,
to lubricate psalms in the chapel; of holiness, to which St Benedict assigned
seven degrees. In her blood was the waking gene, and like her father,

she would glide along dim corridors at night, checking for lights
and fires; blurting a word of solace to herself or some straggler,
alert to the closeness of danger, and of Death coughing his guts up
in the pre-dawn, his body under the blazing Sanctuary light, volted with pain.

Write Yourself in Winter

Go, bridled daughter, from this red-roofed town.
Move past tiny houses set like teeth.
Circle walls of crumbling bone.
Go quickly. Now.
Before evening whispers and shadow women
press you for an answer. Go,
carve your name at the road's fork, on the stump
of broken seasons. Whistle
at March breezes, dress in harebells,
bubbled cider, cuckoo call.
Splinter chapters from the stone-paged book.
Resist its wall-eyed aura of old truth. Listen
to your patron in September, the dead
in November: write yourself in winter.
Snap the single thread that tangles flight.
Move quickly. Angels jostle
to shout 'no' through your mouth.

A-Man-at- a-Bus-Stop sees a Perfect 'O'

Amanatta late night bus stop displays the inside-out grief of those-who-never-had, so
      oh! – never lost, while his fiancée puckers a perfect 'O' with her lips for an

American girl in a silk sheath, descending an amphibious no. 17: cerise
      'O'; teal sheath. The man's eyes, mad with dreams – like beached seals or

ampersands cresting then rock-dashed, colonised,
      open-and-shut in folds of high-rise cheek – see it all:

a mutilated shirt-tail of flapping schoolkids who wrangle
      over a phone; flailing round a tubercular bus-pole which operates as

a mayfoil, while two half-cut lasses
      ogle each other's Amazonian frames:

Amitriptyline-calmed girlfriend (*amore*) amazed and ambivalent, the
      other, out of order, on heat, off her guard and head –

amateurs in steel-coil embrace –
      oh my – making the boys titter.

A.m.
      O – nothing. He declares – and it is for the 1st   (2nd   3rd)   time –

amo

      amo

            amo

Days Round like the Moon

Mapped to the urban (but the soul can live on a little green,
can thrive on a tree; witness Coleridge's patch of sky),
they nonetheless call themselves *women of the blue flowers*,
who flow back to the source, small and pink-breasted, multifoliate,
stamens alight. They will never be obsolete, women of the blue faces,
women of the blue fleeces, their tongues plumped up, giving rue,
dealing it like it was a winning hand at rummy, a many-wristed mother
wiping mouths of bambinos with a muslin napkin while thick white moths
gather at the door. During Compline on the radio, a husband makes a pass
at the agency cook, who takes it all in her athletic stride. At day's end,
the rhythm of the hours pauses on its cusp and the women reclothe
themselves in midnight blue, clutching the stars, women of the blue faeces,
dusting the moon and sinking down naked to dawn and Lauds.

'William lets me wear her ring –'

William lets me wear her ring –
a good brother, our two hearts caudate
and sheepshanked since babyhood.

A grab of gold and emerald
I take it to bed with me and stare at it
by candlelight till the sheen lures me in

and I figure in the greeny-yellow lick
her leaf-mould eyes – her thin waist –
her black rope of hair caught

like a noose on the neck
of an errant stallion –
her bell-voice calling out to

Billy, Billy, for help, but he's stepped aside
to visit with me and is saying, *Dear Sis,
things will be as they were.*

His voice, my own tones back to me,
freezes my *sang-froid*; cauterises
bobbing-girl gladness.

I put her back in the flame's eye
twenty-one times more, murmuring. I tell him
I had a dream and he lifts his soft face to me.

The Dazzle and Flash of New Sheets

I ended up intimate with the notebook.
To begin with, he'd been a perfect brick,
sitting out chill vigils, night after night,
mopping up burblings the fever threw out

in the early hours: quick-fire stutterings
like 'mechanical sunshine', 'chitterlings',
some creature called 'Mashabacka'; the ash,
shelving, from the blaze going on in the bush

in my brain. Then, once, I woke to the gleam
of square shoulders shifting across the room;
was stirred by a pearl oblong torso;
and wriggled, desperate to channel the slew

of phrases loosed from their footings,
demanding a place on the page. Soon, patting
my trunk, amidst fitful dozing, I sensed
the press of his cool flat back at full stretch

on my belly, reading me. He wooed me
with words we'd written together, showed me
the dazzle and flash of new sheets, then lured
me with razzamatazz of steel binding; drew blood.

snow rules

the laws of snow   alter everything
the glamour of frost   drops feather boas

on proud lintels   stone shoulders
of archbishops   and republican heroes

salt-starved Dublin   teeters on ice
the railings a mainstay   for walking unwounded

who cling   I learn the technique
handoverfist   from others

we nod as we pass   chill-bitten
snorting like horses   totting up

how many steps   needed to cross
the ice patina   to the lip of the pavement

a girl at a bus stop   circles the kerb
with the ball of her foot   as if starting a dance

and the boy behind   polishes a spot
to bright glass   preparing a penalty

by tea time O'Connell Street   is hushed and set
with dry white cloths   muffling drifts

of milk powder   monotone 100s-and-1000s
quite distinct   from London's funds of slush

from the bus I see women shuffle   like Japanese ladies:
we draw level, I see clearly   they are Japanese ladies

an African stumbles   and Brazilians samba
outside Café Sol   Poles look bemused

at a city stood still   the radio intones the outlook –
bleak, overcast, dark   with biting winds from the north

displaced and wrong-footed   in a foreign city
I'm lost in *ostranie*   of strange-making snow

the delicate snowflake   has mastered the capital
with tremulous goose feathers   has clogged its throat

Queen Conch Ode

You with your meat as heavy
as half the haunch of a woman.
Cushioned mollusc.
Benthic Bahaman beauty.

Your glossy pink ear –
spiny convolvulus –
flares, yielding pearl:
chatoyant, like moiré silk
in the coral seas
you listen to.

You with your stomach-foot
treading on algae; debris.
Your long egg masses.

Long-liver, you love the lapping shallows,
the falling-away shelved sand of Haiti.
Prized *Strombus* hiding
that lump of edible flesh, fishbait.
Culled for this and for cold
decoration and profit.
Poor poached conch.

Your knuckled shell keeps on thickening
your blood
runs blue with copper.

Rinsed clean, Marine Queen
of the seagrass bed.
With your rose lobes,
your musical bones.

Hasfallen

O has-has-has fallen, mud, muck and dead things.
How bright the Good Children, uniformed
in mulberry, citrus, and cherry.

How they come gusting and fluttering down
corridors, corridors oiled with heartbreaking blue.
How they tremble, swelling their notebooks

with fruitful facts. The previous year's
harvest curves their soft necks.
A drowsy teacher with a copper monocle

blinks mist from her eyes:
wet flaps of sycamore seesaw and shiver
to the beat of songs of old Autumn.

From a locked room a choir whines
and the early caretaker removes sacks
of troublesome mulch, of which nobody speaks.

Goodbye Henna Goodbye

Early autumn I henna'd my hair
blending, a bit, with the leave-taking leaves.

November, I started learning French –
les feuilles mortes.

I composted mince-pies that Christmas,
stroked my thinning hips at Epiphany.

Blue was my favourite colour
in the January sales. A long sarong.

First day of spring I admired the new-painted sign.
Stayed up late checking flat lets in Barnsley.

In a cracked egg-cup,
planted my family tree.

Filled in forms, left-handed. Slid
past a flower seller into a photo booth.

Someone called me by my old name
and I didn't bat an eyelash.

Triptych

In Guildingwells, at Christmastime,
the choristers planned a revolt.

They lit their lanterns early,
wrapped themselves in scarves,

snoods, bobble-hats, balaclavas,
gloves, mufflers, thermal leggings,

and bowled along the lanes, bumping
into hedges and each other

until, climbing the hilltop at the crest
of their valley, star-strung,

and gazing down through the organza
of their breath, at the hour when

once they would have let loose
a volley of song, they turned

to each other, glitter-eyed, silent,
and knelt in adoration.

In Letheringham, in Lent,
lovers restrained themselves by the river,

ducks and geese got by
on bread and water,

retired gentlemen
catechised their wives,

and council workers sought to mortify
hanging baskets,

curbing their flamboyance
with bitter herbs.

In Pontypridd, at Pentecost,
the Holy Spirit peaked

on children who'd played truant,
been scolded, answered back.

Their faces flamed, and words of gold
weighed on their lips.

Their mothers crossed their brows,
aunts eyed them and reported

happenings to the priest, who groaned
deeply, to think of glossolalia on his patch.

Homily of Francis

Preach amber, ambergris, preach sweet pea,
purple sprouting, bread. Preach tourmaline and turquoise,
radish. Preach moon's sprawl, full cream silk,
wind's punch, yellow, storm, pigeon, squirrel,
monkfish and lawn. Peach.
Preach midnight blue, mackerel sky,
pomegranate. Preach cherimoya and budgerigar,
flaked gold harvest. Preach honey skin
and peacock feather, vermilion, passion flower,
lily; preach orange fire and white heat, snow, ice,
cacciatore, asparagus, broken crystal *only*
waterfall, drought, flounce of blossom, *only use*
bunion-roots, crocodile, humming birds, *only use words*
preach pepper, dance. Preach rocky coves *only use words if*
and prairies, parsnip bouillon; the violin *only use words if you*
played in French *only use words if you have to*

The thing about Grace and Laura

was that they were sisters, *vice versas*.
The gentleness of the one, tender
as mousse, flesh like marshmallow;
her demeanour like Turkish Delight;
an apricot, mooning at the sun.

The gunmetal slickness of the other,
her flick-knife wit and belt-buckle
tongue; operating from offices
in the City. I couldn't love
her. A wildcat, out of
control, she stalked me through winters.

Grace slides laughing on her birthday,
her velvet haunches streaked with yellow
from tiger lilies I've placed on her path.
Laura sucks in her cheeks and
intimates that, as per her email,
she won't be celebrating
anything in the current climate.

I edge away
from her coat-hanger glance.

If Grace and Laura were to marry,
that would be incest, anathema.
I covet a calling card for Grace
and she is always welcome.
Laura has me poked to bits
with reminders; red letters.

A Less than Sainted Summer

I can barely pull morning out of the bag,
come August. Our daughters have taken
to wearing serge uniforms
and folding blankets for a living.
The grandparents gurn at passers-by
from windows in their beach huts.
The weekend sunrise looks unconvincing
and there is no 'Oh!' in the ocean.
Uncles adamantly refuse to buy ice creams
for adorably-plaited god-daughters.

My future, a slim thing, languishes
on the leather sofa, with my past, locked
in gossip. My present – a perfect hostess
(puffing, dabbing at moist cleavage)
brings them steaming bronze tea,
shortbread angels, clotted cream eclairs.
A hardness in my heart rubs
against the bedroom furniture.
Vinegary flavours in my gullet
taint the milk. Vapours of aniseed,
elderflower, *Vapona*, link hands and skip.

I'd like to say that Autumn was healing
but it was then that the dead leaves
stayed glued tight
and the house sweated tankfuls.

Edwardiana

An inch or two skimmed from her twill skirt
and the day shaped perfectly in her head:
seamless tennis, swimming, a cycle down the lane
and up, rondeau of elevenses with aunts,
then two loops unhooked from her corset
for patriotic postprandial singing round the piano,
the map of England shaved perfectly on her head.

Strong tea in thin-lipped china, a cake-stand charged
with madeleines and buttered teabreads – mountains! –
shared perfectly by her bed: a long ramble
with a newish lover, in slant-lit gardens,
mallow weighting the air, and under row after row
of high-arching yew, yards and yards
of shadow waiting perfectly up ahead.

Miss Marple loosens her bra,

flicks dust and cottagey debris from the sill
and leans bare elbows through the lattice to catch
a snatch of South Downs air.

A line of sweat down her body's meridian
prickles in response to the breeze.
In the garden rock lilies stand to attention

and a low dog rolls cock-a-hoop in oak shade.
What path of peccadilloes led me here,
she wonders. Beyond the hills

the sea's serrated line seems years away
in the past, memories pickled like salt-kept
winter fish. She fingers a refolded

dearjane letter, always pressed to her person
only today her person seems the wrong
size and shape and there's a licking

restlessness, an itch to shrug off armadillo
shell and wriggle out from tiresome
chasing after clues, lascivious panting

at the door of others' misfortunes.
The grandmother clock strikes four-fifteen.
Miss Marple re-hooks herself

and chugs lavender talc
between her breasts. Cold cuts
and piccalilli, as usual, for tea.

Mise en Gâteau

Last night I dreamt I was a cake, a squat brown gateau
dimpled with cherries above a piped creamy smile. Inside,
falling-away fudge, and smudgy – almost not-baked – sweetness.

I said 'My dear Madeira,' to the lady-cake next door, sister of
Madeleine, *ma belle*: 'Let's dance!'

In the morning, I did that thing of imagining myself as each
ingredient, and myself *mise en gâteau*, dainty and desirable
on my special day, sporting the full meringue, and well-

clabbered. This is the path to reintegration, the dream
therapists say. My inner cake begins to clarify; confect.

The dancers on graves

gather at dawn, 21ˢᵗ June, by the large yew;
limber up, leaning on the back ends of monuments
and tombs; adjust bandeaux and legwarmers;
yodel a little, do scales to loosen the *chi*.

The relevant areas are corralled with ribbon,
beginning with John Henry Frayn, *father of three,*
down to Dawn Mary Highgate, *a friend to all.*
The usual routines, salsa, merengue, rain-dance,

always come out altered on grass, especially
if the going is soft. Some were children when they
started; they say the day fits seamless
into their year. And a lady of 90 (who never forgot

the man who wronged her at seventeen)
performs a perfect foxtrot, resplendent in furs.
The Mercy Brigade, sitting to one side, allocate
marks for flirtatiousness, precision, grace.

Bridal

Your corset, slung across a chair, draws me up short.
Torso of lace, ivory satin, sweetheart bows;
cords of elastic instead of whalebone:
unskirted wedding dress.

How those mock muscles must have hung
slack against your dwindling flesh –
the whole thing billowing –
squaw's tent swirling on a pole.

Like the court shoes you wore for Mass as a girl,
or the winter coat kept on all summer, and all the checks
to sense, which you gradually learned to choose,

much as you taught me – circumcision of the spirit –
so maybe, in the end, it was a comfort to keep the world
in harness, something to push against.

caress

your touch
more darkly-styled
than your kiss
twists
my insides
like table-linen
in the redhanded grip
of Irish washerwomen

a young woman undressed me and

five minutes later she undressed me again
ten minutes after that she undressed me
and again fifteen minutes later
by which time I was beginning to feel tender
her fingers were cool and her palms firm
as she disembarrassed me of one hot layer
after another, tweed, cotton, nylon, loosing
buttons and cuffs, unravelling ties –

when she had been undressing me for a month
I dared to say, sideways, my mouth under the chest
of a pullover which she was easing over my head
with such skill and love that my adams apple
felt like it had been rolled in honey
and rubbed in oats, and my voice was grungy
and low, my skin somewhat shiny
and raw: *muhuuhu muhuuhu ph ph ph hmmhu hm* –

she touched my lip with a shapely thumb: *shhh ...
don't fret.* her voice like jinxed june breezes
in lime leaves. and then. her voice like rills rushing over flint
and dazzling in sunlight. *we'll get you undressed and then
we'll see to that. just a moment now.* and with no let-up still
she continues to undress me

The Very Skin that Hurts

Latterly, I have given the major part of my attention to borrowed billet-doux, procured from a local business on strict condition that I don't try to contact the original correspondent, which is difficult, as I feel he knows me so well and speaks of a vast red tent of love which I think I visited as a girl. He is impeccable in his courtesy and curling script. I sense his points of punctuation like intimate jabs, each one well-judged and yet natural as babble. His tight cravat of grammar. I become obsessed, and when the children are in bed I enter a spacious room with a Regency clawfoot table and maroon leather-backed chairs, where we court, or he courts me, and I let myself fudge and capitulate like before. He is sweet sweet like rolled carob. I bless the ground of my being which he walks over, again and again.

Dora Incites the Sea-Scribbler to Lament

Sees him at the far end of the strand,
squamous in rubbery weed, his knees bobbing
urchins, his lean trunk leaning, sea-treasure for her.

After it all (they mate, like carapaces, in parentheses),
Dora feels coolness in new places, lifts a reused
razor shell, mother-of-pearly and straight

and signals out to the swell of mouldering green.
Dora is electric, in love, and deep water.
Dora, Dora, Dora, in which dread is.

People people the beach, peering
through splayed hands, appealing:
DAW-RAAaargh. A boat sees her passing.

Sea-scribbler's chest buckles
in aftershock – his quill is primed:
squid-inked and witful.

the last thing

they said I should go towards the light –
the last thing I wanted, that all-vacating
white – and I was a stone or two
overweight with tar and muck
I needed more time to work off –
a year, a month, if we're bargaining –
give me a hole, a wet gulley to wait in,
to rinse my tarry shoes, shrive me
and I will consult again
the gold-edged pages of my *Imitation*
the millionstarry oblivion
which made my 13-year-old heart
gallop into gloom – *renounce renounce* –
a startling bouncy break with pain –
blandishments to let go – and in one swoop
the pain stops, while voices far off
drown and I wave as happy
as a spider in lilied bullied twilight

        riddling light comes up to my ankles
        that's okay, you get used to icecapped toes
        damp arches, rheumy metatarsals
        and settle to make sense of dim bookless
        alleyways with their particular latrinalia –
        tearfelt messages in limestone and chert
        demanding headworm logic

and then a flock of patients in an antechamber
whom I am shocked to see need my help
and I am drafted in to place ticks in columns
of a log, to fetch gallons of spilling light
in buckets, fend off curdling flashes

of too black, too jagged, and have people laid
sleeping in my lap while I lift my head
and call out – my palms chafed from batting
cave crickets, sifting pebbles –
sorting them in hollows as they gurgle
and suck themselves downstream
with an adult tang, leaving me clear –
my eyes sore with cataloguing, some dick
in charge bringing more record cards
and warmed laudanum

                               ... I'm chanting psalms
                         looking out for the light again
                         around some sharp corner, exquisite
                         and milk-bright to feed off, but
                         not yet

Acknowledgements

Thanks are due to the editors of journals and publications in which these poems have previously appeared: *Poetry* (Chicago), *The Poetry Review*, *The Best British Poetry (Salt Publishing, 2014)*, *Ambit*, *The Rialto*, *Shearsman Magazine*, *Tears in the Fence*, *Poetry London*, *Magma*, *Under the Radar*, and *Poetry News; Primers Volume 1* (Nine Arches Press, 2016); *Declare* (Shearsman Books, 2016); *Arvon International Poetry Competition Anthology; Norwich Writers' Centre Emerge Anthology; Twin; Resurgence* Poetry Competition anthology 2015, *The Lion Tamer Dreams of Office Work* (ed. A. Bell, Alba Publishing, 2015*)*, *Ver Poets Prize anthology 2016*, and *The Emma Press Anthology of the Sea* (2016). 'Write Yourself in Winter' and 'snow rules' appeared in a Hibernian Writers' Group anthology in Dublin in 2010. 'Triptych' was shortlisted by Carol Ann Duffy in the Arvon International Poetry Competition 2010. 'Miss Marple loosens her bra,' won second prize in the *Ambit* Poetry Competition 2014, and was published in *Ambit* 218. 'Mise en Gâteau' won the 2015 *Magma* Editors' Prize and was published in *Magma* 62. 'Nuala, Nuala, Nightwatchman's Daughter' won second prize in the *Ambit* Poetry Competition 2016 and was published in *Ambit* 226.

I should like to express thanks to Arts Council England for their generous support, without which this pamphlet would not have been completed.

I am grateful also to the Arvon Foundation for bursaries to attend their residential courses, which led to an Arvon/Jerwood mentorship; to Writers' Centre Norwich for an Escalator award; to Julia Bird, and all at the Poetry School, and to Judith Palmer, and all at the Poetry Society, for their ongoing inspiration and support.

Special and heartfelt thanks to Carol Ann Duffy, Patrick Tanner, Kathryn Maris, and all the poets, friends and family who have offered advice, help and encouragement with the poems in this collection.

30 years
of smith|doorstop poets

Moniza Alvi, David Annwn, Simon Armitage, Jane Aspinall, Ann Atkinson, David Attwooll, Anne-Marie Austin, Sally Baker, Mike Barlow, Kate Bass, Paul Batchelor, Suzanne Batty, Zeina Hashem Beck, Chris Beckett, Peter Bennet, Catherine Benson, Gerard Benson, Paul Bentley, Sujata Bhatt, David Borrott, Nina Boyd, Maxwell Boyle, Sue Boyle, Carol Brierly, Susan Bright, Carole Bromley, Sue Butler, Peter Carpenter, James Caruth, Liz Cashdan, Dennis Casling, Julia Casterton, Claire Chapman, Debjani Chatterjee, Linda Chase, Geraldine Clarkson, Stephanie Conn, Stanley Cook, Bob Cooper, Jennifer Copley, Julia Copus, Rosaleen Croghan, Tim Cumming, Paula Cunningham, Simon Currie, Duncan Curry, Ann Dancy, Emma Danes, Peter Daniels, Peter Daniels Luczinski, Joyce Darke, Jonathan Davidson, Kwame Dawes, Owen Davis, Julia Deakin, Nichola Deane, Steve Dearden, Patricia Debney, Mike DiPlacido, Maura Dooley, Tim Dooley, Jane Draycott, Basil du Toit, Christy Ducker, Carol Ann Duffy, Sue Dymoke, Stephen Duncan, Suzannah Evans, Michael Farley, Rebecca Farmer, Nell Farrell, Catherine Fisher, Janet Fisher, Anna Fissler, Andrew Forster, Katherine Frost, Sam Gardiner, Adele Gèras, Sally Goldsmith, Yvonne Green, David Grubb, Harry Guest, Robert Hamberger, David Harmer, Sophie Hannah, John Harvey, Jo Haslam, Geoff Hattersley, Jeanette Hattersley, Selima Hill, John Hilton, Andrea Holland, Holly Hopkins, Sian Hughes, Keith Jafrate, Lesley Jefferies, Chris Jones, Mimi Khalvati, John Killick, Jenny King, Mary King, Stephen Knight, Judith Lal, John Lancaster, Peter Lane, Michael Laskey, Kim Lasky, Brenda Lealman, Tim Liardet, Katherine Lightfoot, Semyon Izrailevich Lipkin, John Lyons, Maitreyabandhu, Paul Matthews, Eleanor Maxted, John McAuliffe, Michael McCarthy, Rachel McCarthy, Patrick McGuinness, Kath McKay, Paul McLoughlin, Hugh McMillan, Ian McMillan, Allison McVety, Julie Mellor, Hilary Menos, Paul Mills, Hubert Moore, Kim Moore, David Morley, Sarah Morris, Blake Morrison, Paul Munden, Daljit Nagra, Dorothy Nimmo, Stephanie Norgate, Christopher North, Carita Nystrom, Sean O'Brien, Padraig O'Morain, Mark Pajak, Nigel Pantling, Alan Payne, Pascale Petit, Stuart Pickford, Ann Pilling, Jim Pollard, Wayne Price, Simon Rae, Irene Rawnsley, Ed Reiss, Neil Roberts, Marlynn Rosario, Padraig Rooney, Jane Routh, Peter Sansom, Tom Sastry, Michael Schmidt, Myra Schneider, Rosie Shepperd, Lemn Sissay, Felicity Skelton, Catherine Smith, Elspeth Smith, Joan Jobe Smith, Cherry Smytb, Martin Stannard, Pauline Stainer, Paul Stephenson, Mandy Sutter, Matthew Sweeney, Diana Syder, David Tait, Pam Thompson, Dennis Travis, Susan Utting, Stephen Waling, Martin Wiley, Tony Williams, Ben Wilkinson, Andrew Wilson, David Wilson, River Wolton, Sue Wood, Anna Woodford, Cliff Yates, Luke Samuel Yates

Laureate's Choice 2015 pamphlets
still available from the Poetry Business

David Borrott | Nichola Deane | Rachel McCarthy | Wayne Price

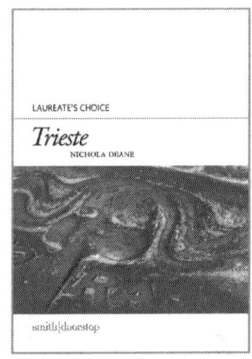

This is a varied but coherent collection, tender, imaginative and clear-eyed. – Carol Ann Duffy

A poet both sophisticated and lyrically charged who deploys imagery that is both precise and daring. – Carol Ann Duffy

Here are bold poems in a collection that is much more than the sum of its mesmerising parts.
 – Carol Ann Duffy

A remarkable new poet who is intelligent, insightful, imaginative and utterly assured.
 – Carol Ann Duffy

£7.50 each or all 4 for £20

www.poetrybusiness.co.uk

Thirty poems to celebrate thirty years of Poetry Business pamphlets

Founded in 1986 on an Enterprise Allowance, the Poetry Business was based for twenty years in a Victorian Arcade in Huddersfield, with poets Peter Sansom and Janet Fisher as co-directors. After Janet's retirement, the poet Ann Sansom took over as co-director and the business moved to its present offices in Bank Street Arts in Sheffield.

For all of those 30 years, we have been publishing pamphlets of one shape or another, starting with Simon Armitage's first published poems in *Human Geography*, right up until the present day with our Laureate's Choice pamphlets by four up-and-coming poets chosen by Carol Ann Duffy.

30 at thirty brings you thirty poems, one from each of the thirty years of the Poetry Business.

£5

www.poetrybusiness.co.uk